Y0-DXJ-716

THE
DEEP
STATE
CONSPIRACY

Does It Exist?

by Eric Braun

Consultant:

Louise Roth, Associate Professor of Sociology, University of Arizona

COMPASS POINT BOOKS
a capstone imprint

Compass Point Books are published by Capstone
1710 Roe Crest Drive, North Mankato, Minnesota 56003
www.capstonepub.com

Editorial Credits
Michelle Bisson, editor; Sarah Bennett, designer; Kelly Garvin, media researcher;
Katy LaVigne, production specialist

Photo Credits
Alamy/Keystone Pictures/USA, 30 (bottom); Getty Images/Bettmann, 19;
Newscom: akg-images, 15, 23, Arnie Sachs/CNP, 26, CARLOS BARRIA/REUTERS,
50, CHINE NOEVELLE/SIPA, 52, Everett Collection, 21, FBI Collection at NARA via
CNP, 27, Jeff Malet Photography, 45, John Barrett/PHOTOlink, 25, JONATHAN
BACKMAN/REUTERS, 11, Joshua Roberts/REUTERS, 46 (bottom), Kevin Lamarque/
REUTERS, 6, LAURA CAVANAUGH UPI Photo Service, 37, Rick Wilking/Reuters,
44, World History Archive, 17; Shutterstock: Benjamin Clapp, cover, Cara-Foto,
12, Casimiro PT, 53 (top), chrisdorney, 14, Christian Delbert, 28, Evan El-Amin, 9,
igorstevanovic, 43, Illustration Forest, 35 (bottom), Jospeh Sohm, 5, 39, JStone, 55
(top), Lenka Horavova, 56, mark reinstein, 46 (middle), 55 (bottom), Numstocker,
38, Onur ERSIN, 18, Rena Schild, 32, Rob Crandall, 46 (top), Shala W. Graham, 40,
Shanvood, 47 (bottom), vnews.tv, 41, zef art, 30 (top)

Design elements: Shutterstock: alanadesign, Ivanova Julia, jumpingsack

**Library of Congress Cataloging-in-Publication Data is available on the Library of
Congress website.**
ISBN 978-0-7565-61734 (hardcover)
ISBN 978-0-7565-62281 (paperback)
ISBN 978-0-7565-61956 (ebook PDF)

Printed and bound in the United States of America.
PA71

Table of Contents

CHAPTER ONE

"THIS IS SO SINISTER" 4

CHAPTER TWO

"SHADOWY ELITES" 13

CHAPTER THREE

"UNSWERVING LOYALTY" 20

CHAPTER FOUR

"FULLY AND COMPLETELY INFORMED" 29

CHAPTER FIVE

"THEY DON'T INTEND TO LOSE POWER" 36

CHAPTER SIX

"I WOULD KNOW. I AM ONE OF THEM." 48

GET INVOLVED 56

GLOSSARY 58

ADDITIONAL RESOURCES 59

SOURCE NOTES 60

SELECT BIBLIOGRAPHY 62

INDEX 64

"THIS IS SO SINISTER"

Like any candidate for political office, Donald Trump made many promises while running for president of the United States in 2016. One of the most important of these was to "drain the swamp." An old rumor about the U.S. capital, Washington, D.C., says that it is literally built on a swamp. It wasn't. But that's not what Trump was talking about anyway.

Besides elected officials, many unelected workers help run the federal government. These workers are hired or appointed. The important jobs they do include enforcing laws,

Fact

About 2.8 million people work in the federal government. Among them are mail carriers, health care workers, park rangers, intelligence agents, and countless others.

investigating crimes, and protecting the health and safety of all Americans. Trump said that many of these people were corrupt. He accused them of working for their own self-gain or being disloyal to the United States. If elected, he would get rid of these bad actors. He would drain the swamp.

Draining the swamp or breaking the government?

After he was inaugurated in January 2017, Trump acted quickly on this promise. Only his definition of "draining the swamp" grew to include more than just dimissing corrupt employees. For Trump, the swamp included just about any person or policy that differed from him in political views. For example, Trump strongly disagreed with the agreement that President Barack Obama had signed with Iran. In this agreement, Iran promised not to develop nuclear weapons. Under the new president, a foreign policy expert in the State Department who was key to helping Obama forge that agreement was demoted to a low-level position. Trump also forced out H.R. McMaster, the national security advisor who favored the Iran deal.

Trump fired James Comey, the head of the FBI, and then fired his replacement, acting director Andrew McCabe. The head of the National Economic Council was pressured to resign after resisting part of the president's trade plan. After Trump determined that his own secretary of state, Rex Tillerson, was not loyal enough, he fired him. The head of Veterans Affairs was also asked to go.

After Secretary of State Rex Tillerson announced that the U.S. and North Korea were about to start negotiations, President Trump tweeted that it was "a waste of time."

The president's conflict with the government went beyond demotions and firings. He slashed budgets. He publicly battled with the Federal Bureau of Investigation (FBI), the Department of Justice, and the Department of State. And when the U.S. intelligence community concluded that Russia had interfered in the 2016 election, Trump said he did not believe it. These Washington lifers, he said, invented their findings to make him look bad.

In March 2017 Trump went even further. He accused former president Barack Obama of spying on him. He said Obama had intelligence agents tap Trump's phone lines during the 2016 presidential campaign. When the intelligence agencies denied it, Trump said they were lying to protect Obama.

A narrative started to emerge. President Trump and his allies in Congress and in the media said that officials working in various agencies of government were trying to sabotage Trump. They said these officials were part of a shadow government known as the deep state. The deep state, according to them, held lots of power. It worked to serve the desires of the political elites—a small group of people who had power, wealth, and privilege. And because those in the deep state were not elected—and were usually anonymous—the American people had no way to check their power.

At first, the president and his team did not use the term *deep state* in public. But it was a popular topic on certain media such as Fox News. Far-right conspiracy outlets including Infowars and Breitbart News Network also discussed it. Internet personalities such as Alex Jones of Infowars told their audiences that the deep state was a threat to democracy.

Fact

Terms such as *left, extreme left, right,* and *far-right* describe the political spectrum. Where people are on the spectrum depends upon their beliefs. Those on the right support more conservative and traditional ideas. They like the idea of having less government involvement. Those on the left believe that all people should be equal, with all the same rights and opportunities. They would prefer to have more government involvement with more guidance and regulations.

What is the obligation of government agencies?

In the summer of 2017, John Brennan, who had been Obama's CIA director, said something that riled up those who believed in the deep state. Brennan said that executive branch officials had an "obligation . . . to refuse to carry out" orders from President Trump if they were harmful or antidemocratic. To many on the political right, this was the smoking gun. It was proof that a secretive group of government officials was working together to undermine the president. In other words, it was proof of a deep state.

Right-wing radio personality Rush Limbaugh was outraged. He said Brennan was calling for a coup—the violent overthrow of government. He said there was a plot organized by "embeds in the deep state at the Pentagon, State Department, and various intelligence agencies." On the Infowars website, Alex Jones echoed fears about a coup. He predicted that Trump would be murdered. Talking about the deep state, he said, "They're saying, 'A month or two we're going to kill the president, month or two we're going to remove him.' This is so sinister."

Fact

Limbaugh and Jones are hugely influential because they reach so many listeners. *The Rush Limbaugh Show* averages about 14 million listeners a week. *The Alex Jones Show* averages almost 6 million. That makes them the number 1 and number 13, respectively, most-listened-to talk radio shows in America.

What was the media's role in creating the idea of a deep state?

By this time, Limbaugh, Jones, Breitbart, and Fox News had been talking about these concerns for months. Their audiences had heard about this so-called shadow government. But by that summer, the idea of a deep state had gained traction in mainstream media as well. And it wasn't just Brennan's comment. Many officials in the executive branch were anonymously leaking secret information to the media. The leakers, and the journalists who reported on them, believed it was important to do so. The American people deserved to know about what they considered Trump's dishonesty or harmful ideas. For example, in August 2017, anonymous employees at the Environmental Protection Agency leaked an important report on climate change. They did so because they feared that the Trump administration would ignore or cover up the report.

The mainstream media and President Trump have had an uneasy, even hostile, relationship from the time of his campaign. That relationship has only gotten worse during his administration.

Many leaks revealed information that was damaging to Trump regarding Russian interference in the election. But to Trump and his supporters, this was more evidence that a shadow government was working against him. Trump included the mainstream media in the definition of deep state. Reporters had relationships with government officials and often reported stories that made Trump look bad. Trump called the media "the enemy of the people."

Trump and his team had been talking among themselves about the deep state since before the election. Trump's chief advisor, Steve Bannon, didn't just believe in the deep state. He wanted to destroy it. To him, the deep state represented everything that was wrong with Washington. It was old power. It was the establishment. Nothing could change in politics until it was dismantled.

Conspiracy or reality?

To others, the idea of a secret government that was really in charge sounded unrealistic. The deep state was a conspiracy theory cooked up by far-right rabble-rousers. They wanted an excuse for why Trump was facing so much opposition. It was true that Trump was dealing with more leaks than any recent president. One report said leaks came out seven times faster during the first few months of Trump's presidency compared to the same time period of the presidencies of Obama and George W. Bush.

But this was not because of any deep state, many argued. It was simply the state—the government in its

Who Is Steve Bannon?

A former naval officer, Steve Bannon graduated from Harvard Business School in 1985 and started a mergers and acquisitions company that specialized in media and entertainment. He sold his company in 1998, and in the 2000s he made political documentaries. One was about former Republican president Ronald Reagan. Another was about Sarah Palin, the former Republican vice presidential candidate.

In 2012 Bannon took over as executive chair of the conservative Breitbart News Network after its founder, Andrew Breitbart, died. Bannon forged an even more conservative image for the network, gaining a strong following among people on the far right. This included white nationalists, also known as white supremacists.

Bannon became the chief executive of Donald Trump's presidential campaign in the summer of 2016. By fueling fears of immigration and distrust of Trump's opponent, Hillary Clinton, Bannon led the campaign to a surprise victory. He took his far-right nationalist agenda to the White House as the president's senior advisor. He is credited with influencing much of Trump's antiestablishment agenda in his first months as president. But when Bannon was later quoted as criticizing a Trump meeting with Russians during the campaign, he was fired by the president.

purest form. The government is supposed to work that way.

David Remnick, writing in *The New Yorker*, said, "Previous presidents have felt resistance, or worse, from elements in the federal bureaucracies." He continued, "Eisenhower warned of the 'military-industrial complex'; L.B.J. felt pressure from the Pentagon; Obama's Syria policy was rebuked by the State Department." If Trump was facing more resistance than other presidents, it was because that resistance was needed, Remnick wrote. So many of his actions were bad for the country. His secrecy about his relationship with Russia—a U.S. enemy—was alarming. It was the job of civil servants to protect the U.S.

What should Americans make of all this? Is there really a deep state? And if so, what is it exactly?

Do You Believe in the Deep State?

In spring 2017, a news poll asked Americans if they believed that there are "military, intelligence, and government officials who try to secretly manipulate government policy." The results were:

17%
don't know

48%
deep state exists
(28% think it's a major problem)

35%
only a conspiracy theory

Source: https://abcnews.go.com/Politics/deep-state/story?id=47086646

CHAPTER TWO

"SHADOWY ELITES"

Historically, the term *deep state* has been used to describe secret groups operating inside authoritarian countries. More specifically, it refers to networks of military and intelligence officers as well as civilian allies in developing countries. Examples include Algeria, Pakistan, Egypt, and Turkey. These societies were officially democratic. But really, the elected leaders were not in charge. Generals and spies were. Historians sometimes refer to these people as "shadowy elites."

Egypt and Turkey are recent examples of countries with deep states. In those countries, the deep state has used violent means to maintain control over elected officials. That includes riots, coups, and assassinations. The democratically elected president of Egypt, Mohammed Morsi, was eventually ousted in a coup in 2013. In Turkey, the deep state has worked against President Recep Tayyip Erdogan for years. But he was able to surround himself with allies to keep power. After a failed coup attempt in 2016, he jailed, deported, and killed many dissidents.

Clearly, the United States does not see this kind of violent resistance. Elected officials are rarely assassinated. There aren't coups. Citizens don't see tanks in the streets. But the U.S. does have a history of its intelligence agencies abusing power for their own ends.

The FBI evolved from previous versions of federal law enforcement agencies in the 1930s. It is in charge of domestic security and intelligence. This includes criminal investigations, counterterrorism, and counterintelligence. The National Security Act of 1947 established the Central Intelligence Agency (CIA) to focus on foreign intelligence. The National Security Agency (NSA) was established for similar reasons in 1952.

Fact

Early in World War II President Franklin D. Roosevelt was getting piecemeal intelligence from various sources. He established the Office of the Coordinator of Information (COI) to streamline the process. It was led by World War I hero General William "Wild Bill" Donovan. Over the next several years, the COI changed and grew. Eventually it evolved into the CIA.

Who were they spying on?

The business of all these agencies was, in large part, spying on people. That worried a lot of Americans. The agencies worked in secret. Who would make sure the agencies were acting in good faith? It would be easy to abuse their power to spy on people. For a democracy to work well, it is important for the government to be open. Citizens need to be able to see and understand what its government is doing. That way they can vote for officials who do things they like, and vote against those who don't. That's why a free press is so important. The press keeps a closer eye on government than most people have the time or expertise to do. Then they report the news to the public.

Having secret agencies went against all that. And indeed, intelligence agencies did abuse their power. Sometimes they worked in cooperation with their elected superiors to gather intelligence on, and damage, political enemies. Every president from Franklin Delano Roosevelt through Richard Nixon used the intelligence community to spy on politicians who opposed them. FBI director J. Edgar Hoover spied on Americans suspected of being communists and those who expressed opinions against the U.S. government. He also spied on protesters, radical student groups,

J. Edgar Hoover

gay people, and others. To do this, the FBI used wiretaps and bugs to listen to people's conversations and phone calls. They opened people's mail and broke into their homes. The NSA collected international communications made by Americans suspected of acting against the United States.

The information they gathered uncovered some people's worst secrets. It was used to bribe, threaten, and discredit

The FBI's "Suicide Letter" to Martin Luther King Jr.

FBI director J. Edgar Hoover worked for decades to discredit civil rights leader Martin Luther King Jr. In 1961 the FBI learned that King had become close friends with former Communist Party insider Stanley Levinson. The FBI began spying on Levinson and later on King. Around the same time, King began to publicly criticize the FBI. He said Hoover was deliberately letting southern police officers get away with racist acts and policies. He said Hoover wasn't enforcing civil rights laws.

Hoover's spying never revealed any communist activities by King. But the FBI did learn that King was unfaithful to his wife. In November 1964, King and his wife, Coretta, received a package. It contained an audio tape that was apparently a recording of King with other women. The letter called King "evil" and "a colossal fraud" and other nasty names. It threatened to expose King's infidelity to the nation. The writer concluded by saying, "There is only one thing left for you to do. You know what it is."

Though the letter was anonymous, King suspected it came from the FBI. The "one thing" they wanted him to do, he assumed, was kill himself. Years later, it was confirmed that the FBI had sent the letter.

Recent FBI director James Comey kept a copy of the King wiretap request on his desk. It was a reminder of how the bureau had done wrong—and still could.

them. The FBI broke up marriages and friendships. It ruined people's careers and reputations. One of the more famous examples of the FBI going too far relates to Martin Luther King Jr. The FBI spied on King for years. Hoover and others hoped to find out if he had communist ties, among other things. They never found any.

J. Edgar Hoover ran the FBI for almost 50 years. He built up the bureau as a law enforcement arm, but his abuses of power led to the limitation of FBI director terms to 10 years.

Why spy?

But sometimes the intelligence agencies worked *against* elected officials. Agencies did this to further their own interests and influence policy. The main weapon for this type of abuse was leaking secret information to the media. Officials would secretly gather information about politicians and leak it or threaten to leak it. Here, too, Hoover was a master. He secretly collected embarrassing or incriminating information on executive officials, senators, and members of Congress. Then he let them know he had it. Politicians did what Hoover wanted them to do in order to keep their secrets.

The FBI also used leaks to shape the story of a certain policy or make certain politicians look bad. These leaks were not always accurate. They sometimes portrayed

The idea of a deep state conspiracy in the United States might've started with Hoover's FBI agents, who ignored the Constitution when they spied.

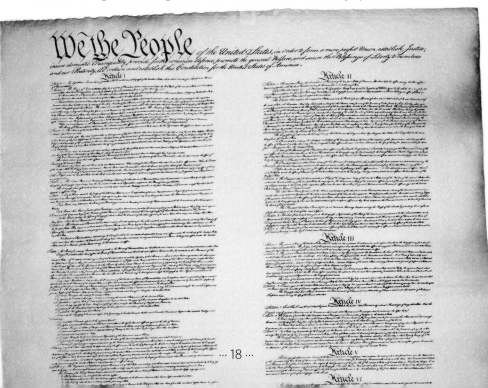

"distorted, exaggerated facts" to get the support they wanted for a particular action.

There were two main reasons this kind of abuse was able to happen. First, there were virtually no laws regulating intelligence agencies. William Sullivan was in charge of domestic surveillance under Hoover. According to him, agents simply ignored the Constitution—the primary law-giving document of the United States.

The second reason was the secrecy. Not only were there no laws governing intelligence gathering, but Congress wasn't really watching over these agencies. In fact, members of Congress often told intelligence officials *not* to let them know what they were doing. Even within the agencies themselves, there was little oversight. It was a recipe for corruption.

William Sullivan (right) was head of domestic surveillance under J. Edgar Hoover. Sullivan helped give rise to the idea of a deep state by stating that his agents simply ignored the law in pursuit of their targets.

CHAPTER THREE

"UNSWERVING **LOYALTY**"

One of the most important examples of abusive use of power comes from the decades after the end of World War II. In these years, the Soviets began testing nuclear weapons. The Soviet Union became secretive. It blocked itself off from the rest of the world behind physical boundaries known as the Iron Curtain. American citizens Julius and Ethel Rosenberg were convicted of spying for the Soviet Union.

Fact

The Rosenbergs were executed for treason on June 19, 1953. They maintained their innocence until the day they died.

Ethel and Julius Rosenbergs' two sons led a decades-long campaign to prove that their parents were not spies. Recent evidence suggests otherwise.

During this time, American fear of communism spiked. But communist ideas remained popular among a small number of Americans on the political left, especially labor leaders and intellectuals. In the U.S. House of Representatives, a committee on "un-American Activities" already existed. Its job was to investigate anyone suspected of being disloyal or working against the United States. Communist spies who had been caught testified before the committee that the Soviets had spies in U.S. government.

In 1947 President Harry S. Truman created the Federal Employees Loyalty Program. It established political-loyalty review boards to determine the "Americanism" of federal government employees. The boards recommended the firing of un-American employees. This decision was often made with little evidence.

Six years later, President Dwight Eisenhower issued an executive order. It declared that "all persons privileged to be employed in the departments and agencies of the Government, shall be reliable, trustworthy, of good conduct and character." It went on to say that everyone in the government must have "unswerving loyalty to the United States." A new government agency, the Bureau of Security and Consular Affairs, was created to enforce this order.

How could you tell who was loyal?

This bureau investigated Americans suspected of disloyalty. The House un-American Activities Committee conducted character investigations of many Americans. So did other committees led by Senator Joseph McCarthy of Wisconsin. McCarthy gained a prominent public platform through these committees. He used his position to rail against communism.

How were these suspected disloyal Americans found and investigated? They were spied on. Intelligence agencies tapped phone lines and secretly opened people's mail. They used hidden microphones and other secret devices.

As a result of these activities, many workers in the State Department were determined to have communist sympathies. They were fired or arrested. This was often done without evidence—or with exaggerated or invented evidence. If the agencies didn't have the proof to get rid of someone they didn't like, they made it up. After all, nobody was watching over them.

Fact

In March 1950 a political cartoonist invented the term *McCarthyism* after the actions of Senator McCarthy. It is still used to mean accusing a political opponent of subversion or treason without evidence.

Senator Joseph McCarthy, on little or no evidence, accused hundreds of State Department employees of being disloyal to the U.S. government. He also claimed that communism was spreading across the nation, again with little or no evidence.

The paranoia and political persecution of this era came to be known as McCarthyism. It shows what can happen when intelligence agencies and elected officials work together in secret without regard for the law.

Years later, another high-profile abuse of intelligence was exposed. Here, too, a source in the executive branch leaked secret information. In this case, he was working against an elected official—the president of the United States.

The Influence of Watergate on the Idea of the Deep State

It started on June 17, 1972. Five men were arrested while breaking into offices inside the Watergate office building in Washington, D.C. The offices belonged to the Democratic National Committee (DNC). The DNC was campaigning for the Democratic candidate for president, George McGovern. The criminals were working for the Republican candidate, President Richard Nixon. They were photographing Democratic Party documents and tapping the phones.

After the arrest, an investigation uncovered more related crimes. The men were identified as Republican operatives, but the question of who ordered the break-in was unclear.

Then a reporter at the *Washington Post* received a helpful tip from a knowledgeable source. The reporter, Bob Woodward, and another reporter, Carl Bernstein, had been covering the story. But they hadn't made much progress figuring out how widespread the conspiracy was. The tip led them in the right direction.

Woodward knew the informant. He was a high-ranking official in the FBI. But Woodward kept the man's identity secret from everyone except Bernstein. Over the next several months, the two reporters got more information from the source. They published more stories. When the source wanted to meet Woodward to give him information, he had a secret way to let him know. He would circle a page number in the reporter's copy of *The New York Times* and draw a clock with the hands indicating a time. Woodward and his source usually met in in the bottom level of an underground parking garage.

Bob Woodward (left) and Carl Bernstein were young reporters when they broke the most important story of their generation.

Woodward and Bernstein's reporting eventually pointed to the involvement of the executive branch. Someone in the White House, perhaps even the president himself, had directed the break-in and many other illegal activities.

The administration had bugged the offices of political opponents. It had used the intelligence agencies to spy on individuals and groups it was suspicious of. After the men were arrested at the Watergate building, Nixon worked to cover up his administration's involvement.

Woodward and Bernstein's reporting led to a major scandal and crisis. The president was investigated by Congress and faced impeachment proceedings. He resigned before he could be impeached.

Surrounded by his family (wife Pat, daughter Tricia, and son-in-law Ed Cox) Nixon resigned the presidency on August 9, 1974.

The White House had been using the intelligence community as a political weapon. But it was an employee in that community who was key to Nixon's downfall. Nixon and his administration may have gotten away with huge crimes if the secret informant in the FBI had not provided clues and information to the reporters to guide their investigation.

Woodward and Bernstein kept the identity of their source secret for more than 30 years. In 2005 former associate director of the FBI Mark Felt revealed himself as the informant. He was worried his fellow FBI agents and others would think of him as a traitor. But by this time, most Americans considered the source an American hero and patriot. He had put his career and personal safety at great risk in order to expose corruption at the highest level of U.S. government.

Mark Felt was the second in command at the FBI at the time of Watergate. He was passed over for the top spot at least in part because Nixon suspected him of being the leak.

Fact

Bernstein and Woodward wrote about their experience working with the secret source and reporting on Watergate in a book. It was titled *All the President's Men*. The book was made into a movie in 1976. It was nominated for eight Academy Awards and won four, including Best Adapted Screenplay.

The Dual State

In 1955 a political scientist wrote an article about Eisenhower's executive order and the activities of the Bureau of Security and Consular Affairs. Hans Morgenthau did not yet know that the bureau was using its power to spy on Americans. But rumors were persistent. In his article he said that secretive intelligence gathering, and condemning people based on that intelligence, goes against how a democratic government is supposed to work.

He said there was a *dual state* in the U.S. government. One level of the state was the legitimate government, which was elected and had the power to make laws. On the other level were *agents of the secret police*. These agents could use power to influence or veto decisions made by the elected government.

Morgenthau's phrase, *dual state*, was an early version of today's *deep state* as many use it now. It meant national security agents were using secretly collected intelligence to influence the actions of elected officials.

CHAPTER FOUR

"FULLY AND COMPLETELY **INFORMED**"

Abuses by government insiders, both in cooperation with elected officials and in defiance of them, went on for decades. FBI director J. Edgar Hoover, Senator Joseph McCarthy, and President Richard Nixon were three main examples. But many other stories had come out by the mid-1970s. These included information about secret U.S. plans to assassinate foreign leaders and disrupt foreign governments. There were stories about agencies spying on American civilians and then tracking their political activities.

Finally, in 1975, the Senate formed a committee to investigate abuses of intelligence. The Church Committee was led by Senator Frank Church of Idaho. It found a lot

The Church Committe Report led to major reforms in how intelligence agencies were allowed to gather and use information.

of troubling information. A big one was that major U.S. telecommunication companies had been sharing phone records with the NSA. The NSA used this information to form a watch list. The list had millions of names and biographical information of people the NSA wanted to monitor. It included famous actors, lawmakers, writers, and many others.

The Church Committee published its findings in the Church Committee Report in 1976. The report made many of these abuses public, though some of the committee's findings remained secret at the request of the CIA.

The Church Committee and Congress

These findings led to important reforms that permanently changed the way U.S. intelligence agencies can operate. The president and the intelligence agencies were allowed to keep doing surveillance, including spying on American citizens. But now Congress was granted strong oversight. Congress got to put restrictions on how the agencies and the president collected and used information. Domestic surveillance required a court order. Both the Senate and the House of Representatives formed intelligence committees. These committees had to be kept "fully and currently informed" about intelligence activities. Inspectors monitored the agencies to make sure they were obeying the restrictions.

Have these reforms been effective? In many ways, they have. A massive leak of secret government information in 2013 affirmed that. On May 20 of that year, a computer programmer who worked as a subcontractor for the NSA took a leave of absence from work. Edward Snowden told his supervisor that he had a health problem. But before he left, he copied a huge trove of top-secret documents about NSA surveillance practices. Snowden wasn't sick. He got on a plane and left the country with the stolen data saved to a thumb drive.

Snowden flew to Hong Kong, China, where he met with journalists from *The Guardian*, a newspaper based in the United Kingdom. He gave the journalists the information he had stolen. The files showed a large domestic spying program that Snowden found disturbing. The day after the meeting, *The Guardian* and the *Washington Post* released the information. Many people were as disturbed by the reach of the spying program as Snowden was. Many others were furious with Snowden for betraying American secrets.

The domestic spying that Snowden revealed was controversial and shocking. It was also possibly illegal. But the documents showed that the branches of government were working together. The documents didn't show any examples of intelligence agencies or others working on

Protesters rallied against mass surveillance during an event organized by the group Stop Watching Us in Washington, D.C., on October 26, 2013.

their own, in secrecy, or against the elected branches of government. Many people believe this shows that the reforms brought on by the Church Committee have been effective in that way.

But Snowden's leaks didn't only reveal massive domestic surveillance. They also exposed international spying operations, which were perfectly legal. Making these secret actions public damaged international relations and revealed the identities of sources. The U.S. military later claimed that Snowden's actions may have caused billions of dollars in damage to its security structures.

Was Snowden a whistle-blower or a thief?

The U.S. charged Snowden with theft of government property and unauthorized communication of national defense information. It also charged him with "willful communication of classified communications intelligence information to an unauthorized person." To avoid going to prison in the U.S., Snowden now lives in Russia. He is unable to return home or even leave the country because the U.S. revoked his passport. But despite this, he believes he did the right thing and that it was worth the personal risk. "I'm willing to sacrifice [my former life] because I can't in good conscience allow the U.S. government to destroy privacy, internet freedom and basic liberties for people around the world with this massive surveillance machine they're secretly building," he said.

So it appears that the Church Committee Report ended certain abuses by unelected government officials, particularly those in intelligence agencies. These agencies no longer seem to use their powers to blackmail or threaten elected officials to gain power over them. We do not see presidents or senior executive officials using intelligence agencies to attack political enemies. So, intelligence has not been used by government officials to gain political power.

We do see leaks of classified information to the press. But these have consistently been for the purpose of holding elected officials to the standards of a democracy. This type of leak puts a spotlight on corruption or illegal activity. Leaks in recent years have exposed illegal interrogation or torture, deadly use of drones, and questionable surveillance activities. Once illegal or legally questionable acts are made public, Congress can act to stop or change them. And it has done so over the past few decades.

Intelligence Timeline

1935   The FBI is established, with J. Edgar Hoover named as director.

1945   World War II ends.

1945   The House Committee on un-American Activities becomes permanent.

1947   The CIA is established.

1947   President Truman creates the Federal Employees Loyalty Program.

1950   On February 9 Senator McCarthy gives a speech naming "enemies within" the government. He begins vigorously investigating government employees to test their loyalty.

1952   The National Security Agency (NSA) is established.

1953   President Eisenhower establishes the Bureau of Security and Consular Affairs to ensure all government employees have "unswerving loyalty to the United States."

1953   Julius and Ethel Rosenberg are executed for spying.

1955   Political scientist Hans Morgenthau coins the phrase *dual state*.

1972   Republican operatives are arrested for breaking into Democratic offices in the Watergate office building on June 17.

1974   President Nixon resigns after reports in the *Washington Post*, aided by leaks from a secret government source, show that he used the power of the presidency to spy on opponents and obstruct the investigation into Watergate.

1975   The Church Committee, led by Senator Frank Church, is formed to investigate intelligence abuses.

1976   The Church Committee Report makes public vast abuses by intelligence agencies and reforms are put in place.

2013   Edward Snowden leaks a trove of secret government documents revealing massive domestic and international spying operations.

CHAPTER FIVE

"THEY DON'T INTEND TO LOSE **POWER**"

Citizens' concerns about unelected power go back to the earliest democracies. The Roman statesman Cicero spoke of a government within the government. In modern democracies, concerns about the influence of lobbyists, business interests, and career government bureaucrats are common and reasonable. Democratic government doesn't work well if some people or groups have more influence than others.

Conservatives on the far right have recently been the most vocal about hidden powers. But the idea of a secret government has caught the fancy of people of various political beliefs. After the terrorist attacks of September 11, 2001, intelligence and security efforts in the U.S. grew to massive levels. It seemed to many, especially on the left, that the spying and security agencies were not accountable to laws or elected officials. The military and intelligence agencies similarly seemed to work in extra-legal secrecy. This included private defense contractors hired by President George W. Bush's administration. Some on the left even believed that Bush was behind the terrorist attacks as a way to profit off Iraqi oil.

To many, the sheer mass of the surveillance exposed by Edward Snowden was evidence of unchecked government power. Snowden himself agreed. "There's definitely a deep state," he told an interviewer in 2014. "Trust me, I've been there."

Is there really a deep state in the United States?

Until recently, the term *deep state* was rarely used. That changed with the rise of Donald Trump. In December 2016, after Trump was elected president, the Breitbart news site ran a story titled "The Deep State vs. Donald Trump." In it, the author asserted that the established powers hated Trump. They wanted to keep his administration ineffective. They may have lost the election, he said, but "they don't intend to lose their power" to an outsider like Trump. This may have been the first time Trump's establishment enemies were collectively called the deep state in a large media outlet. The deep state, the Brietbart writer said, would do anything it could behind the scenes to hurt him. The goal was to "block the President-elect, or at least to discredit and de-legitimize him, such that his presidency is crippled."

Concerns about unelected power may have been common before. But using the term *deep state* changed the tone of these concerns. *Deep state* is menacing. It suggests more than a few civil servants or lobbyists trying to get their way. It implies secrecy, efficiency, and far-reaching influence. It suggests ruthless control from a team effort. We picture civil servants, lobbyists, businesses, and the mainstream media all working together for a common goal. In the eyes of the far right, that goal was simple: Destroy Trump.

Even before he was elected, Trump planted seeds about hidden powers working against him. When he spoke of "draining the swamp," he was talking about those behind-the-scenes sources of influence in Washington.

This promise tapped into the fears of many Americans who didn't trust the government. For them, it was easy to believe that the government was filled with corruption and secret influence.

In fact, Trump claimed the election was rigged against him. He said if he did not win, it was because hidden powers did not want him to win. It was not hard for his followers to imagine that this was true. Of course an established power structure would want to keep a disruptive force like Trump out of Washington.

The Role of the Resistance

When Trump did win, there was a powerful reaction against him. Citizens from all sectors of society, including some in government, expressed fear and anger about the president-elect. Trump won the electoral college but he actually lost the popular election by 3 million votes. Many voters felt that the real will of the people had been denied.

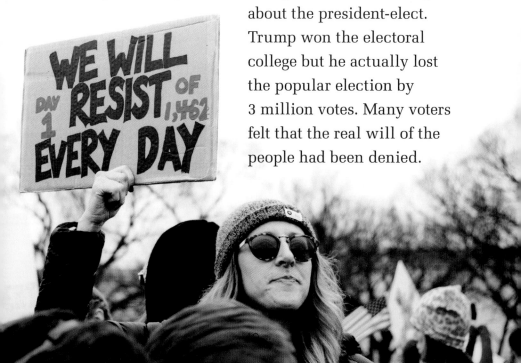

As soon as Donald Trump was elected president, people began to protest against him. They believed that he promoted racism and cruelty.

They saw his policy ideas as cruel and helping only the wealthy. His personality and style were reckless and dangerous. He had acted in sexist, racist, and selfish ways. A president Trump was scary and disheartening to many.

The movement against Trump took on a name: the Resistance. To those who opposed him, especially those who were politically liberal, resistance made sense. It wasn't a conspiracy. It was a logical reaction to a dangerous president. But Trump and his supporters saw the Resistance as the deep state refusing to give up its power to an outsider.

Voices on both sides grew louder. And things escalated once Trump was inaugurated in January 2017. President Trump didn't disguise the fact that he was hostile to much of the government he now led. His chief strategist, Steve Bannon, was considered the mastermind behind Trump's rise and his agenda. Bannon said that the administration would be engaged in a battle for "deconstruction of the administrative state."

STAY EDUCATED AND STAY INVOLVED

OUR RESOURCES

MOST RECENT UPDATES

GREEN AND GLOBAL: MARCH 12TH-29TH

STRIKING, SAVING, SPEAKING, SPARKING: FEB. 28TH-MARCH 12TH

BLACK HISTORY MONTH 2019: A LIST IN TWO PARTS

The Islamophobic attack in New Zealand, Background Check Expansion Act, climate walkouts & the Green New Deal, and school segregation in NYC. Read more.

Info on worldwide youth climate strikes, the Domestic Gag Rule, the Save the Internet Act, a border update, and vaccine bills in state assemblies. Read more.

A two part list for Black History Month featuring history and action. Read more.

Teens Resist

The resistance to Donald Trump was deep and came from all parts of society, including young people. Brooklyn teens Sonia Chajet Wides and Kate Griem formed a youth-advocacy website in October 2017 called Teens Resist. The site gives regular updates on issues important to young people in the Resistance. This includes gun control, immigration, and LGBTQ rights. Teens Resist also provides inspiration, advice, and calls to action.

The goal, according to Wides and Griem, is "to make political activism accessible to passionate youth in a world where their voices matter more than ever."

The two had campaigned tirelessly for Democratic candidate Hillary Clinton. They were devastated when she lost to Trump. Worried and angry about the future of their country, the two teens decided to turn their concerns into action. They felt they had the tools, the desire, and the need to do something. After all, they said, "The world shaped by politicians and activists now is the world where we will grow up."

And as Trump's term began, it did seem he was working toward that goal. He undermined his intelligence agencies. He fired or criticized important government officials. He didn't fill vacant positions, leaving important agencies understaffed and overwhelmed. He criticized foreign allies and praised enemies. Virtually everything he did was a rebuke of the established state.

Public institutions began to fight back even more. Individuals in government secretly leaked information about Trump's administration. For example, they leaked his discussions with foreign leaders or his plans for executive actions. Anonymous people in public institutions created Twitter profiles. These included workers in the National Park Service, NASA, and even within the White House itself. They used the public platform to criticize the president.

Trump and his allies believed this fighting back was even more evidence of the deep state. They lumped mainstream media into the conspiracy. The media often reported on the risks or possible illegality of the president's actions. Trump accused them of being "fake news." So did the pro-Trump conservative media. When employees from the Environmental Protection Agency leaked the report on climate change to *The New York Times*, Breitbart News published an article titled "Deep State Teams with Fake News."

Russia, Hacking, and the Election

At the same time all these things were going on, Americans also learned that Russia had interfered with the 2016 election. Directed by Russian president Vladimir Putin himself, the efforts were wide-ranging and very effective. Hackers stole private emails from the Democratic Party and published them. Russians created almost 500 profiles on social media to spread fake news. They worked to heighten people's fears and confirm their biases. Russia even had a spy secretly join the National Rifle Association (NRA) to influence its political actions. The NRA is a powerful political group.

According to extensive evidence gathered by U.S. intelligence agencies, the Russians worked hard to get Donald Trump elected. It was well known that Putin and top officials hated his rival, Democrat Hillary Clinton. Evidence also shows that they have business relationships with Trump and his company.

The debates between Trump and Clinton during the 2016 campaign were hostile. The two candidates repeatedly made rude comments about one another.

President Trump denied that he had any help from the Russians. In fact, he went against what his intelligence leaders told him. He said he did not believe that Russia affected the election at all. He said all the talk about Russian influence was just another way the established powers were working against him. They wanted to make his election look illegitimate.

Fact

Russian social media didn't only work to directly support Trump. Some profiles pushed more liberal alternatives to Hillary Clinton such as Bernie Sanders and Jill Stein. They knew that it would be nearly impossible to convince liberals to vote for Donald Trump. So they worked to get them to vote against Clinton.

In March 2017 FBI director James Comey testified before the House Intelligence Committee. He said that the FBI had not only been investigating Russian influence. It was also investigating possible connections between

In March 2017 FBI director James Comey testified before Congress about Russian attempts to influence the 2016 campaign in favor of Donald Trump.

Trump expressed anger at Sessions for recusing himself.

It was feared that Trump would fire Rod Rosenstein for hiring a special counsel.

Robert Mueller's Russia investigation was conducted without leaks.

the Trump campaign and the Russians. Were they working together? Trump denied this, and in May, he fired Comey. At first the White House said Attorney General Jeff Sessions recommended the firing because of poor job performance. But in a later interview, Trump said it was because of "this Russian thing." He added, "I faced great pressure with Russia. That's taken off."

Attorney General Jeff Sessions had contact with the Russian ambassador when he was a senator. So he recused himself from any investigations involving Russia. That responsibility then fell to Deputy Attorney General Rod Rosenstein. He appointed a special counsel to investigate Russia's influence on the election. The special counsel was also to investigate Donald Trump's possible connection with that interference. And, because of the reasons Trump gave for firing Comey, he was to look into whether Trump was trying to stop the investigation.

Rosenstein appointed Robert Mueller, a former head of the FBI, as special counsel. Democrats in Congress strongly supported Mueller's investigation, as did many Republicans. But the investigation, run by unelected officials in the government, gave those who believed in the deep state new ammunition for their argument.

President Trump's Approval Ratings

As with any president, Trump's approval ratings have fluctuated in reaction to many factors. However, most presidents may see very high highs and low lows. But Trump's base—his core supporters—tends to approve of him no matter what's in the news. That gives him a "floor" of about 36 percent approval. That's where it was at the start of the investigation. His approval soon rose to the low 40s, where it has stayed for months. It remained the same after the end of the investigation.

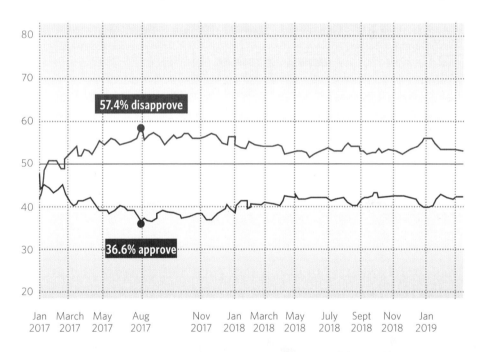

Source: https://projects.fivethirtyeight.com/trump-approval-ratings/

CHAPTER SIX

"I WOULD KNOW. I AM ONE OF THEM."

The Mueller investigation lasted nearly two years. As it continued, criticism from the political right became constant. Conservative voices in the media called it a witch hunt and a waste of money. They consistently called for an end to the investigation.

President Trump was also openly critical of the investigation. He regularly tweeted jabs at Mueller, Democrats in Congress, and the idea of his colluding with Russia. He often peppered his tweets with the phrases "No collusion!" and "Witch hunt!" The president's allies in Congress joined in criticizing the investigation. They labeled it a corrupt conspiracy against Trump.

In fact, Trump claims it is Hillary Clinton and Democrats who should be investigated. Clinton used a personal email server during her time as secretary of state years earlier. This may have exposed classified information to hackers. Trump further claims that it is in fact Clinton who worked with the Russians during the 2016 election. The FBI investigated her extensively during the election. They said there was no reason to prosecute her for her emails. Using a private server was careless but not illegal. It has not investigated her with regard to Russia, saying there is no evidence to support the claim.

But Trump and others claim she should have gone to prison. To Trump, the fact that she hasn't been prosecuted is proof that holdovers from the Obama presidency are protecting Democrats. And that they are out to get him.

What was going on with the swamp?

By 2018, the so-called swamp had apparently gotten worse—even though the Republicans were in power. And Trump had been elected to drain it. The swamp was being portrayed as a super-intelligent, multi-armed enemy of the president. The definition of the deep state had grown beyond intelligence officials. It now included a wide collection of connected players in other administrative agencies, in private industry, and in the media.

That year, Fox News commentator Sean Hannity became the most influential TV and radio personality in the country. A Trump ally who reportedly talks to the president every night after his broadcast, Hannity regularly criticized the so-called deep state. Millions of viewers tuned in to Fox News every day, where the deep state conspiracy was discussed as fact. Talk of the deep state had become a money-maker. Several conservative writers published books about the deep state.

Sean Hannity has said he is not a journalist and, therefore, sees no ethical conflict in choosing sides. He openly campaigns for President Trump.

Just when it seemed that talk of the deep state could not get any more heated, an article in *The New York Times* stirred the controversy even more. On September 5, 2018, the *Times* published a column by an anonymous "senior official in the Trump administration." The official claimed that there is a secret resistance movement surrounding Donald Trump.

Steady state resisters
or deep state conspirators?

The article was titled "I Am Part of the Resistance Inside the Trump Administration." In it, the official described that resistance. "Many of the senior officials in his own administration are working diligently from within to frustrate parts of his agenda and his worst inclinations."

"I would know," the writer went on. "I am one of them."

There was one big reason the writer gave for publishing the piece. Given the chaotic behavior of the president and his administration, "Americans should know that there are adults in the room." The author said Trump's "misguided impulses" were "detrimental to the health of our republic." He said that members of Trump's team had even talked about invoking the 25th Amendment. This amendment provides for the removal of a sitting president if he is considered incompetent or mentally incapable.

The author anticipated how conservatives would react and tried to head it off. "This isn't the work of the so-called deep state," the writer said. "It's the work of the steady state."

That did not stop deep state theorists from making their arguments. Trump was described as "volcanic with rage." He tweeted that the author was "GUTLESS." He also questioned whether there even was such an author. Perhaps the "failing *New York Times*" had made it all up. If the person did exist, he demanded that the *Times* turn him or her over to the government.

The writer's distinction between the "so-called deep state" and the "steady state" gets to the heart of the argument of whether the deep state exists. It is clear that many individuals in and out of government have opposed Trump and parts of his agenda. The president and his allies argue that this is evidence of the deep state working against him. Others argue that this is simply the way government is meant to work. After all, President Trump has radically changed government and broken down norms. And during his first two years in office, his party was not only in charge of the executive branch, but also both houses of Congress. To address that lack of balance, many protesters took to the streets. Others decided to run for office to try to take back Congress from Republican control. The Democrats won the House in 2018 and now the balance of power has shifted. Many who oppose Trump are recently elected representatives.

Nancy Pelosi, new Speaker of the House (center, in gray coat), poses with the 89 female Democratic representatives of the 2019 Congress, many of whom were elected for the first time in 2018.

Tweet 35500 **Following** 45

Donald J. Trump ✓

@realDonaldTrump

45th President of the United States of America 🇺🇸

Tweet Tweet

Donald J. Tru
...Hopefully we
that we are no

President Trump's Tweets

The president primarily uses Twitter to speak to the public, especially about issues that anger or frustrate him. Here are some highlights of his usage from May 17, 2017, the date on which Robert Mueller was appointed special counsel, through the end of 2018.

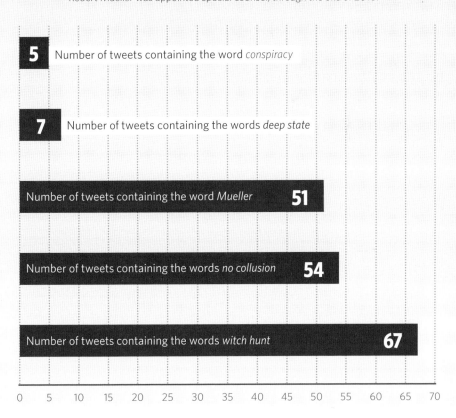

5 Number of tweets containing the word *conspiracy*

7 Number of tweets containing the words *deep state*

Number of tweets containing the word *Mueller* **51**

Number of tweets containing the words *no collusion* **54**

Number of tweets containing the words *witch hunt* **67**

0 5 10 15 20 25 30 35 40 45 50 55 60 65 70

Another argument against the existence of the deep state has to do with its size. Popular conspiracy theories imply a big underground organization working together toward a common goal. But the U.S. government is a huge entity with many individuals working in it. These fragmented groups don't communicate and don't all know each other. They don't have a unifying goal. They don't and can't act as one single force to "take down" a president.

On the other hand, they do act in ways that protect their own interests. In a way, the president is right that the individuals in government agencies often disagree with the person in charge. Many people consider this to be a good thing. As law professor Jon D. Michaels wrote in the journal *Foreign Affairs*, "Officials inside these agencies can defend environmental and workplace safety standards, international alliances, and the rule of law. They can investigate, document, and publicize instances of high-level government [wrongdoing]."

The reason they can do that is largely because they are protected from political pressure. They can't be voted out for doing something that might be right but unpopular.

Investigation Results

Many conservatives attacked the Mueller investigations for several reasons. For one thing, they have criticized the cost. Reporting shows that the investigation had cost about $25 million as of late 2018. On the other hand, it had taken in about $48 million. The money it has earned has come from seizing assets, levying fines, and collecting unpaid taxes.

Another criticism of the investigation has been that it was a witch hunt—a hunt for imaginary targets. But Robert Mueller and his team uncovered many criminal activities and corruption. They initiated criminal proceedings against dozens of people, many of whom have been indicted and sentenced. This includes several members of Trump's campaign and three Russian organizations.

Critics have said the investigation is politically biased, as many members of Mueller's team are Democrats. But both Mueller and FBI deputy director Rod Rosenstein, who appointed him, are Republicans.

Paul Manafort (below), who ran Trump's presidential campaign for months, was sentenced to prison for obstruction of justice and tax evasion, among other crimes.

Michael Cohen (above), Trump's personal lawyer, was sentenced to three years of prison for crimes including arranging payments to silence women during the 2016 campaign who alleged they had affairs with Trump.

GET INVOLVED

Arguments about the deep state conspiracy—like nearly all partisan issues—can be loud, angry, sensational, and loaded with wild claims. How can you know what to believe? Media literacy is the ability to identify and understand the different types of messages we receive. Just like regular literacy—the ability to read and write—you can practice this skill and get better at it. When you do, you learn to think critically and be a smart consumer of information.

Media messages come in countless forms. Traditional media include newspapers, books, radio, and TV shows. There are also YouTube videos, websites and online ads, social media, video games, and memes. Even the packaging on the products you buy, like food and toys, contains media messages.
And every message you receive has something in common. Someone created it, and they did it for a reason.

To be a more savvy consumer of media, ask yourself these questions when you see a media message.

Who created this?

Was it an individual person? Was it a company? How do you know? Go a step further and research the author or company to see if you can find out more about their motives.

Why was it created?

What is the author's goal? Is it to get you to buy something? Is it simply to inform you? Is it to change your mind about something? Is it to entertain you? How does the creator benefit from you consuming this message? How do you know?

What is the creator doing to make the message stronger (more believable, more persuasive, funnier, etc.)?

Does it use techniques such as quotes from experts or statistics from a reliable source? Is there strong evidence? Does it have an authoritative voice? Do you find it believable? Why or why not?

Is the information balanced?

Are some important details or ideas left out? Are opposing views left out? Especially if it is a partisan or polarizing topic, figure out if you need to find a different source to get a fuller understanding. How can you tell? Be careful of confirmation bias. This is the tendency we all have to believe messages that confirm our preexisting beliefs.

After you have considered the answers to these questions, think about how you feel about the message. Do you think most people would agree with you? Would some disagree? Why or why not?

GLOSSARY

collusion—a secret agreement or cooperation especially for an illegal or dishonest purpose

conspiracy—a secret plot created to achieve an evil or deceitful purpose

corruption—dishonest or illegal behavior by people with power

counterintelligence—the collecting of political or military information from an enemy in order to keep them from gathering intelligence or to deceive them

coup—the violent overthrow of a government by a small group

deconstruction—breaking down or analyzing something to find out its true significance

dissident—a person who disagrees with or works against a government

domestic—something that happens within one nation

elite—a person who has lots of power because of his or her position

embed—a person attached deeply in a group such as a government

impeachment—the act of removing someone from office

inauguration—a ceremony to begin an official's term in office

incriminate—show proof of a person's role in a crime

intelligence—information gathered about an enemy or potential enemy

recuse—to remove oneself from participation to avoid a conflict of interest

Resistance—the movement against President Trump

subversive—behaving in (often secret) ways that undermine a government

ADDITIONAL RESOURCES

Critical Thinking Questions

When U.S. intelligence agencies were created, many people worried that they would become corrupt because they operated in secrecy with little oversight. Do you think secret, unchecked power will always become corrupt? Why or why not?

What do you think about Edward Snowden's decision to leak secret U.S. information about domestic and foreign spying? Are there times when it's okay to leak secret information and times when it's not? What's the difference?

Why do you think some people believe in the deep state and others do not? What does a person's belief about the deep state say about their other beliefs?

Further Reading

Brockenbrough, Martha. *Unpresidented: A Biography of Donald Trump*. New York: Feiwel and Friends, 2018.

Colich, Abby. *FBI Agents*. North Mankato, MN: Capstone Press, 2018.

Honders, Christine. *Watergate and the Resignation of President Nixon*. New York: Lucent Press, 2018.

Hudak, Heather C. *McCarthyism and the Red Scare*. New York: Crabtree Publishing Company, 2018.

Internet Sites

Consortium for Media Literacy
www.consortiumformedialiteracy.org

Media Education Lab: Curriculum Materials
mediaeducationlab.com/curriculum/materials

Teens Resist
www.teensresist.com

SOURCE NOTES

p. 8, "obligation … to refuse…" Michael Crowley, "The Deep State Is Real," *Politico*, September/October 2017, https://www.politico.com/magazine/story/2017/09/05/deep-state-real-cia-fbi-intelligence-215537 Accessed February 25, 2019.

p. 8, "embeds in the deep state…" Ibid.

p. 8, "They're saying…" Aidan Quigley, "DEEP STATE IS 'GOING TO KILL THE PRESIDENT,' ALEX JONES CLAIMS," *Newsweek*, August 4, 2017, https://www.newsweek.com/alex-jones-says-deep-state-going-kill-president-646802 Accessed February 25, 2019.

p. 12, "Previous presidents have felt…" David Remnick, "There Is No Deep State," *The New Yorker*, March 20, 2017, https://www.newyorker.com/magazine/2017/03/20/there-is-no-deep-state Accessed February 25, 2019.

p. 19, "distorted, exaggerated facts…" Jack Goldsmith, "Paradoxes of the Deep State," *Can It Happen Here? Authoritarianism in America.* Cass R. Sunstein, Ed., New York: HarperCollins Publishers Inc.: 2018.

p. 22, "all persons privileged…" Ibid.

p. 32, "Snowden is a spy…" Twitter: Donald Trump, https://twitter.com/realdonaldtrump/status/457314934473633792?lang=en Accessed February 25, 2019.

p. 33, "I'm willing to sacrifice…" Biography: Edward Snowden, https://www.biography.com/people/edward-snowden-21262897 Accessed February 25, 2019.

p. 37, "There's definitely a deep state…" "The Deep State Is Real."

p. 38, "block the President-elect…" "Virgil: The Deep State vs. Donald Trump," Breitbart, December 12, 2016, https://www.breitbart.com//virgil-the-deep-state-vs-donald-trump/ Accessed February 25, 2019.

p. 41, "deconstruction of the administrative state…" Charles S. Clark, "Deconstructing the Deep State," *Government Executive*, Nd, https://www.govexec.com/feature/gov-exec-deconstructing-deep-state/ Accessed February 25, 2019.

p. 42, "to make political activism accessible...The world shaped..."
Sonia Chajet Wides and Kate Griem, "Teens Resist Was Created by
High Schoolers to Help Youth Engagement in Politics." *Teen Vogue*,
August 24, 2018.

p. 46, "this Russian thing..." Matt Apuzzo, Maggie Haberman, and
Matthew Rosenberg, "Trump Told Russians That Firing 'Nut Job'
Comey Eased Pressure From Investigation," *The New York Times*, May
19, 2017, https://www.nytimes.com/2017/05/19/us/politics/trump-rus-
sia-comey.html?login=smartlock&auth=login-smartlock
Accessed February 25, 2019.

p. 51, "Many of the senior officials..." Anonymous, "I Am Part of the
Resistance Inside the Trump Administration." *The New York Times*,
September 5, 2018, https://www.nytimes.com/2018/09/05/opinion/
trump-white-house-anonymous-resistance.html
Accessed February 25, 2019.

p. 54, "Officials inside these agencies..." Jon D. Michaels, "Trump and
the 'Deep State'," *Foreign Affairs*, September/October, 2017, https://
www.foreignaffairs.com/articles/2017-08-15/trump-and-deep-state
Accessed February 25, 2019.

SELECT BIBLIOGRAPHY

Books

Goldsmith, Jack. "Paradoxes of the Deep State," in *Can It Happen Here? Authoritarianism in America*, Sunstein, Cass R., ed. New York: HarperCollins Publishers Inc., 2018.

Websites and Articles

Anonymous, "I Am Part of the Resistance Inside the Trump Administration," *The New York Times*, September 5, 2018, https://www.nytimes.com/2018/09/05/opinion/trump-white-house-anonymous-resistance.html Accessed February 25, 2019.

Clark, Charles S., "Deconstructing the Deep State." *Government Executive*, https://www.govexec.com/feature/gov-exec-deconstructing-deep-state/ Accessed February 25, 2019.

Crowley, Michael, "The Deep State Is Real," *Politico Magazine*, September/October 2017, https://www.politico.com/magazine/story/2017/09/05/deep-state-real-cia-fbi-intelligence-215537 Accessed February 25, 2019.

Feffer, John, "What Trump Means by the 'Deep State'," Institute for Policy Studies, August 30, 2018, https://ips-dc.org/what-trump-means-by-the-deep-state/ Accessed February 25, 2019.

Grandin, Greg, "What Is the Deep State?" *The Nation*, February 17, 2017, https://www.thenation.com/article/what-is-the-deep-state/ Accessed February 25, 2019.

Michaels, Jon D, "Trump and the 'Deep State'," *Foreign Affairs*, September/October 2017, https://www.foreignaffairs.com/articles/2017-08-15/trump-and-deep-state Accessed February 25, 2019.

Nunberg, Geoff, "Opinion: Why The Term 'Deep State' Speaks To Conspiracy Theorists," NPR.org, August 9, 2018, https://www.npr.org/2018/08/09/633019635/opinion-why-the-term-deep-state-speaks-to-conspiracy-theorists Accessed February 25, 2019.

Osnos, Evan, "Trump vs. the 'Deep State'," *The New Yorker*, May 21, 2018, https://www.newyorker.com/magazine/2018/05/21/trump-vs-the-deep-state Accessed February 25, 2019.

Remnick, David,"There Is No Deep State," *The New Yorker*, March 20, 2017, https://www.newyorker.com/magazine/2017/03/20/there-is-no-deep-state Accessed February 25, 2019.

Sommerlad, John, "Deep state: Is there really a secretive 'shadow government' working to undermine Donald Trump?" *Independent*, September 7, 2018, https://www.independent.co.uk/news/world/americas/us-politics/deep-state-donald-trump-conspiracy-theory-alex-jones-steve-bannon-alt-right-a8525521.html Accessed February 25, 2019.

Struyk, Ryan, "What you need to know about the 'deep state'," ABC News, April 29, 2017, https://abcnews.go.com/Politics/deep-state/story?id=47086646 Accessed March 31, 2019.

Virgil, "The Deep State vs. Donald Trump," Breitbart, December 12, 2016, https://www.breitbart.com/politics/2016/12/12/virgil-the-deep-state-vs-donald-trump/ Accessed February 25, 2019.

Wolf, Z. Byron, "There may actually be a 'deep state.' It's just not the one Trump fears," CNN, September 6, 2018, https://www.cnn.com/2018/09/06/politics/steve-bannon-trump-conspiracies/index.html Accessed February 25, 2019.

About the Author

Eric Braun is the author of dozens of books for kids and teens on many topics including sports, money smarts, and overcoming mistakes. He is not a member of the deep state, but he is deep. He lives in Minneapolis with his wife, two sons, and a dog named Willis.

INDEX

Bannon, Steve, 10, 11, 41

Bernstein, Carl, 24–25, 26, 27

Brennan, John, 8

Bureau of Security and Consular Affairs, 22, 28, 35

Bush, George W., 10, 37

Central Intelligence Agency (CIA), 8, 14, 30, 35

Church Committee, 29–30, 33, 34, 35

Clinton, Hillary, 11, 42, 44, 45, 49

Comey, James, 6, 16, 45–46

confirmation bias, 57

Congress, 7, 18, 19, 21, 26, 31, 34, 45, 47, 48, 52

domestic surveillance, 19, 29, 30, 31–33, 35

Eisenhower, Dwight D., 12, 22, 28, 35

elections, 6, 10, 40, 44–46, 48–49, 52

Federal Bureau of Investigation (FBI), 6, 14, 15–17, 18–19, 24, 27, 35, 45, 47, 49, 55

Federal Employees Loyalty Program, 21, 35

Felt, Mark, 27

Griem, Kate, 42

Hannity, Sean, 49–50

Hoover, J. Edgar, 15, 16, 17, 18, 29, 35

House un-American Activities Committee, 21, 22, 35

Jones, Alex, 7, 8, 9

King, Martin Luther Jr., 16, 17

leaks, 9–10, 18, 24, 27, 31–33, 34, 35, 43

Limbaugh, Rush, 8, 9

McCabe, Andrew, 6

McCarthy, Joseph, 22, 23, 29, 35

media, 7, 8, 9, 10, 11, 15, 18, 31, 34, 35, 38, 39, 43, 48, 49–50, 50, 51, 56, 57

Morgenthau, Hans, 28, 35

Mueller, Robert, 47, 48, 53, 55

National Rifle Association (NRA), 44

National Security Agency (NSA), 14, 16, 30, 31, 35

Nixon, Richard, 24, 26, 27, 29, 35

Obama, Barack, 5, 6–7, 8, 10, 12, 49

political spectrum, 7, 47, 52, 55

Putin, Vladimir, 44

Resistance, 41, 42, 50, 51

Roosevelt, Franklin D., 14

Rosenberg, Ethel and Julius, 20, 35

Rosenstein, Rod, 46, 47, 55

Russia, 6, 10, 11, 12, 33, 44–46, 48, 49, 55

Sessions, Jeff, 46

Snowden, Edward, 31, 32, 33, 35, 37

social media, 32, 43, 44, 45, 48, 51, 53, 56

Soviet Union, 20, 21

special counsel, 46–47, 48, 53, 55

spying, 6–7, 15–17, 20, 21, 22, 26, 28, 29, 31–32

Sullivan, William, 19

"swamp," 4, 5, 39, 49

Truman, Harry S., 21, 35

Trump, Donald, 4, 5–7, 8, 9–10, 11, 12, 32, 38, 39–40, 40–41, 42, 43, 44–46, 46, 47, 48–49, 50, 51, 52, 55

Twitter, 32, 43, 48, 51, 53

Watergate, 24–27, 35

Wides, Sonia Chajet, 42

Woodward, Bob, 24–25, 26, 27